THE NEW MOM'S GUIDE TO

Finding Your Own Mothering Style

THE NEW MOM'S GUIDE TO

Finding Your Own Mothering Style

Susan Besze Wallace
with Monica Reed, MD

Revell

a division of Baker Publishing Group
Grand Rapids, Michigan

Published by Revell
a division of Baker Publishing Group
P.O. Box 6287, Grand Rapids, MI 49516-6287
www.revellbooks.com

Printed in the United States of America

Library of Congress Cataloging-in-Publication Data
Wallace, Susan Besze, 1969–
    The new mom's guide to finding your own mothering style / Susan Besze Wallace with Monica Reed.
        p.   cm. — (The new mom's guides ; bk. 4)
    ISBN 978-0-8007-3301-8 (pbk.)
    1. Mothers. 2. Mother and infant. I. Reed, Monica, M.D. II. Title.
HQ759.W313 2009
649'.122—dc22   2008038511

Published in association with the literary agency of Alive Communications, Inc., 7680 Goddard Street, Suite 200, Colorado Springs, CO 80920.

Contents

Contents

Introduction

Feeling Comfortable
in Your New Role

My first son never liked to lie flat on his back. Even when he was already asleep, the second I put him down on his back, he'd squirm and fuss and fuss and fuss. But he slept like a rock in the car.

So one night, during those overwhelming first weeks home, in that dark-of-night desperation, we brought the car seat to the cradle. Propped up and strapped in as though he were shuttling to the moon, he conked out.

For five months, his bedtime routine was our secret. I was too anxious and embarrassed to mention it to the pediatrician. I knew it wasn't hurting him, but surely I was doing something wrong. Right?

The bathroom fan was another magic sleep aid. The gentle roar soothed my little boy in seconds and protected his sleep—in the car seat, of course—from our barking dog and ringing phone. Sometimes it would hit me, as I thought of my child sleeping in the bathroom: *my baby sleeps in a place where people pee!*

Many months later, a good friend mentioned that if her baby fell asleep while they were out for a walk, she rolled her jogger stroller right into the house and into the bathroom, and she flipped on the fan to prolong the nap.

I'm not crazy. I'm not alone. Hearing her strategy was like getting a verbal hug.

It takes time to find your parenting groove, to gain confidence in what you know about your child—and feel okay asking when you haven't a clue. You do it all over again with each newborn.

But your first child sends you through uncharted waters as you contend with the opinions, interest, and expectations of parents, in-laws, and old friends. Advice pours in from all corners.

Being a new mom is like being at the helm of a ship for the first time—through occasionally stormy seas and with many well-meaning first mates trying to tell you their own sea tales as you steer. Unexpected buoys cause you to veer one way or the other. Sifting through what friends say is right, the way your mother did it, or maybe the way you wish she had, can send you reeling. Getting your sea legs takes time, and it takes patience with yourself and others. New parents have to learn what to filter, what to try, and how not to offend others in the process.

It's important to remember that you *are* this child's mom. You may not have every trick and technique in your arsenal yet, but you have a set of sensitivities and sensibilities that you will build on, or deconstruct. That's the journey of motherhood.

As you venture forth, your circle of friends will shift. Your connection with your parents and in-laws will hopefully mature. Your time for others will change. And who you *want* to have time for, well, that may change too.

Surrounding yourself with love and laughter and steadfast support during the early mothering years is crucial. By sharing this adventure—in all its glory and with all your goofs—you can become a better mom, you can be held accountable for your choices, and you can truly enjoy this wonderful season of life. By going it alone—or with superficial relationships—you are shortchanging yourself and your children.

You are raising a child but also growing a mother's heart, mind, and soul. Welcome to the next chapter in your life story.

Rearview Mirror

What You Bring with You

A woman is a walking, talking scrapbook, a collage of memories, experiences, and probably some tattered edges too. You reflect where you've been and whom you've been there with or without. For two or three or even four decades you've been this work in progress. And now it's your turn to shepherd and shape a new life.

Sounds pretty daunting in the postpartum days, doesn't it, when just getting a diaper secure on that tiny tush is a challenge? It *is* daunting, and taking the time to think about who you are as a mother, and who you want to be, is very important. The busy wind of parenting can sweep away all your goals and good intentions if you haven't anchored them in your heart.

It's easy to dismiss the infant era as one your child won't remember, but it's the perfect time to establish your values and your goals—your game plan. Before you know it, you'll be hearing a little voice that reflects yours. Little feet will be padding along behind you. You want the path they follow to be intentionally set.

Recently my three little boys were having a postdinner, prebath boogie party—spastically break-dancing in their underwear and diapers. They were bouncing off each other, laughing as loud as the blaring music. This is a pretty common scene in my household—the dancing, the laughing, and yes, the underwear. Growing up with two fairly docile sisters, I often stop my own dancing to marvel at the mass of mini-manliness before me. But on this particular evening, a different thought stopped me. I wondered, *Is this*

"Cooking with my children
will always be important to me because of how
fun I thought it was to be around the kitchen
when I was a child.

I was the third child, so being trusted with a role,
helping *create* something—
even if it was only setting the table—meant a lot.
Private time with one parent
was really big.

Going to work with my dad,
working in the garage with him,
or going on an early morning fishing trip—
those things made our relationship
outstanding."

Lisa

one of those things they'll always remember about their childhood?

I sure hope so. Laughter, parents who aren't afraid to shake their own booties in a show of family solidarity, a love of music—yes, I hope so.

What do you treasure from your childhood? A place? A feeling? An experience? How can you put those good memories into play for your own children?

I grew up in a very suburban neighborhood with parents who adored nature. Each Christmas season all five of us squeezed into the front of my dad's work pickup and drove more than an hour to a Christmas tree farm. We'd run around leaving hats or scarves on the trees with potential. My mom's tree preference, always fat and full, usually prevailed. Dad wielded the saw. Some years it was bone-chilling cold. One year my dad got stopped for speeding. We always stopped at Dairy Queen for lunch. I can still feel the shoulders of my family

"My mom, though she worked all day, consistently followed through with family dinner at the table every night. No matter how hectic her day or how ordinary the meal, at the same time we all prayed and ate. I want that for my family and I'm realizing how very difficult that is nowadays."

Kim

in the seat of that truck. Tradition, togetherness—there was no question these would become hallmarks of my parenting.

My grandparents lived in a tiny dollhouse of a home. Most of the rooms were precise and immaculate and not too child-friendly. It was hard to get comfortable. But I was always drawn to the sewing room, which welcomed me with a pegboard wall blanketed with family pictures. My mom and her sisters' black-and-white wedding portraits hung at the top, the rest of the images seeming to fall from the unions they represented.

I loved gazing at that wall. A feeling of security washed over me in that room—it was one I belonged in. Probably as a result, family photographs are my favorite art. I splash my kids' faces everywhere and hope that a sense of belonging and security pervades every square inch of our home, no matter what it looks like or where it is.

"My parents expected a lot of me, and I learned to be very responsible and goal oriented. But my mom had me when she was twenty-one and then had my sister fourteen months later. At different points in my life I realized she had us close together because she wanted to 'get it out of the way.' She couldn't wait for us to grow up and be self-sufficient so that she could have her life back. The summer before I went to college, she turned my bedroom into a workout room, and I slept on an air mattress in the living room until I moved out. I want my kids to know that I enjoy every minute of every stage they are going through. When you are buried in diapers, bottles, tantrums, and housework, sometimes it's hard to make the most of each day and spend quality time with your kids instead of always looking to the future. But in that way I want to be different from my mom."

Terra

We should view parenting as a backpack we fill with the necessities—clothing, food, shelter—but one that comes with hundreds of little pockets in which to tuck the true stuff of survival: unconditional love, generosity, humor. What would you pack for your kids? What was in your parents' backpack that shaped your childhood?

My dad was always a stickler for honesty. And now I find that even a little lie out of my boys makes me crazy. Also, my folks let me find my own way many times, with attempts at hobbies I wasn't suited for and boyfriends that should never have been. Learning the hard way is sometimes the best way. It's a challenge not to hover over our kids, whether toddler or teenager, but I'm grateful that independence was nurtured in my childhood.

There will always be things we wish our parents had done differently. Now that you are a mom, sleep-deprived and full of ache for how much you want to give your little person, you will probably have more empathy for your folks and be more forgiving of the things you hope not to repeat. If becoming a parent hasn't already opened your eyes very wide to the past, it will.

It's more productive to learn from your childhood than rehash it. For example, my parents never talked to me about sex. The week of my wedding I playfully asked my mom if she was going to have "the talk" with me. She blushed and said she thought that if I had any questions, I'd ask. I think it was characteristic of her generation to be reserved, if not silent, about such personal matters. I don't hold it against her, but I do plan to be in my kids' faces with information on the topic.

My friend Kris said her mother kept her faith, and many emotions, very private. So Kris is intentional about lying down with her kids at night, reading, talking through the day, and especially sharing with them her reliance on God.

"The same year I left home, my brother also moved out to pursue his career, and the **reality of both of her children being gone** for good sent my mother into a deep, ugly depression. She chose to lash out at me particularly, claiming that my lack of closeness with God was the sole cause of the strain on our relationship. The bond with my mom is still strained. **But as a mom now myself, I have a much greater appreciation** for what she and my father did right as parents. My goal as a Christian mother is to **meet my children right where they are, just like God does with us.** It will be hard not to have high expectations for their choices and even harder to watch them make their own journeys in life. But when they fall—I want to be there to **welcome them with open arms and a nonjudgmental heart.**"

Elizabeth

You may have been hurt deeply by the actions or attitudes of a parent, a pattern you've sworn not to repeat. Sometimes you need help to follow through on those intentions.

"It took me nine years to realize that some of the things I was doing as a parent were hurtful, things I'd learned from my mom," one friend said. "I wish I'd considered that earlier, but when you are raised a certain way, you don't know better.

"It was all about control in my house growing up," she said. "For that reason I will never make food an issue. If you don't like dinner, have a yogurt. And if you want to post your art on your bedroom wall, go for it."

There's a possibility that becoming a parent could unearth some sadness in you stemming from your childhood experiences, or it could reopen the wounds of grief from losing a parent. Consider talking with a counselor if these feelings are weighing heavily on you. Your baby needs the best of you. Taking good care of yourself emotionally, physically, and spiritually is a great example to start setting.

Finding Your Mothering Style
Taking Stock

1. What do I hope to instill in my children that is a reflection of my own childhood?

2. What does my husband bring to our kids from the way he was raised?

3. What do we hope to do differently than our parents did?

It's All
Relative

Dealing with the Grandparents

It was cold. I was exhausted, and I was with my mother-in-law, my out-of-town sister-in-law, and my newborn son, attempting a shopping outing. My brand-new stroller would not open. I had no idea what I was doing. We fiddled. We banged. Inadvertently we scratched the heck out of the stroller tray on the asphalt, creating permanent scars that remind me of the first time I felt inept as a mom in front of my mother-in-law.

It was certainly not the last time. During the writing of this book, I found myself in tears when, out of the blue, my son, a preschooler, decided he didn't want to go to school. He ran away from me

"When I think of the relationship
between a kid and a grandparent,
I think there's nothing out there quite like it.
It's unique.
It's a beautiful thing.
And yet an in-law relationship—
with these same people—
can be one of great struggle."

Noell

through the building and took a swat at me when I tried to retrieve him. For twenty minutes I tried to regain a sense of calm for us both, trying to figure out what to do and what lesson this experience would teach. My in-laws, one of whom works at the school, both arrived during my breakdown. Within five minutes my son was sauntering off to class—with them.

I was mortified and humbled—and many other things. Luckily I adore my in-laws. They are loving, faithful, fun people who give without hesitation. Later that day I was able to tell them how lame I felt as a mom that morning, how empty of answers. I didn't mention that after fourteen years of being married to their son, I still seek their approval. Heck, I still seek my own parents' approval.

Having children changes the shape of your relationship with your parents and your in-laws. Hopefully it will deepen those bonds and enrich them through the shared joy of watching a child grow up. But bumps along the way are normal.

Opinionated grandmas, the unspoken dynamics of grandparent child care, and their indulgent gift-giving practices can all cause a rift in your relationship. As a new mom you have a great opportunity to prevent problems in these areas by talking them through early on.

When a mom or mother-in-law offers advice—maybe the way she fed or napped her kids—it's likely she's just trying to help. Even if she is indeed *trying* to make you feel inferior, you should still handle it the same way—with respect and a thick skin.

"You've certainly been there."

"I appreciate your perspective."

"I'm just trying to get my bearings."

"I'll definitely think about that."

"As a grandmother of seven and a mentor mom to a Mothers of Preschoolers group, I have seen that you can really hamper a relationship with your mother-in-law by not being open and honest. I know it's easier for a mother and daughter to communicate— in many cases at least. But if you start out the right way, honest and respectful, it will do wonders. Also, if you go into any relationship with low self-esteem or insecurities— as a mother-in-law, daughter-in-law, mother, or daughter—you're not going to be on the same page. You have to think about who you are and what's behind your feelings."

Jeanine

"I sure am doing the best I can."

"I guess we're always learning."

There are two things at work here: your intense desire to do things right and her desire to be useful in her grandchild's life. If you can break out of *your* role for a minute, it's easier to appreciate hers. I have a friend, a mom of four kids under ten years old, who says she spends a lot of time thinking about her future grandchildren. She's trying to raise her kids to raise *them*, so she strives for gentleness and accountability. She's trying to raise *herself* to be a grandma who doesn't have any regrets about the way she parented, so she doesn't bring along any baggage. It's an admirable, forward-thinking perspective.

It's important to remember these are evolving relationships with your baby's grandmas. Their connection with your kids will grow as your kids do. If something feels off, you can likely change it if you are honest and gentle. That's especially true with grandparents who live close enough to babysit.

"My mom is almost a daily part of my kids' lives. However, she has had to understand that they are ultimately *my* kids, and although she is free to give advice, I won't always take it," Sheridan said. "I also have to be considerate of my parents and not expect them to be built-in babysitters. My mom will watch them whenever I ask, but I try to have other sitters so that my kids never become a burden to her."

Once I saw a sign that said, "What happens at Nana's stays at Nana's." As a new mom, I was insulted by that message. *This is my precious baby—nine months of work and worry before he even got here! You can't change my strategy when I'm just starting the game!* How far I have come! I still hold fast to my ideals but can let go of unnecessary, or imagined, power struggles.

Starting out, you have to decide what really matters. For example, I don't think an occasional donut is going to hurt my child's diet as much as it's going to help create memories with a grandparent. But I have several friends who are livid when their kids are fed junk by their grandfolks. Your call. All moms have their nonnegotiables, and they should. If my parents or in-laws can't stick to my preferred bedtime, I really have to ask myself, what's the cost this time? If we have big plans the next day, I say so in advance and try to provide every head start I can to help them have a smooth evening together. If bedtime was rough or a child decided not to eat, it's not the end of the world. I'm just grateful for the break, and we might try a different strategy next time. Having a friendly conversation about these things *before* you leave a child in a grandparent's care can go a long way in creating peaceful child-care transitions for all of you. Hopefully over time your

"I always say to my mom, 'Guess I need to keep having babies if I want to get you here more often,' because I know she'll come for a newborn. I grew up with grandparents nearly across the street, and I always imagined my mom would visit all the time. I just want her to see all the cute little everyday things my kids are doing, to really know them. My mother-in-law lives five hours away, and recently she was here and let my husband and me go Christmas shopping. She spent two hours in my daughter's room, just talking. My daughter showed her every necklace, every treasure. I want my own mom to experience that."

Cristal

children will come to understand that they get indulged and loved in different ways in different places.

"I have learned to give specific instructions on what I'd like done," Elizabeth said. "It was important to explain to my mom and mother-in-law that some things have changed, like laying baby on his back versus stomach, from when we were babies. I even gave my mom a pamphlet from the hospital."

Kim said one painful evening actually paved the way for good communication with her in-laws. Here's what happened at a restaurant when they were celebrating a birthday with extended family:

"My husband, Matt, and I had been struggling with our son sitting in a high chair while we were eating dinner. He would much rather get out and roam from person to person or climb in a lap. We had been fighting this for a while and had just recently made a strong effort to be consistent. A short time after we sat down, Colby decided he wanted up. Matt's dad offered his lap, at which point we told him we really needed Colby to stay in his chair. Matt's mother began to get upset because we were not getting him out. After what felt like forever to me with an unhappy, crying child, I looked over to see Matt's dad putting his hands out, gesturing 'Come to me. I'll hold you.' Down a few more chairs Matt's mom is beginning to cry because our son is being forced to stay in his chair.

"At that point, I'd had enough. I stood up and said, 'We're leaving now.' Dinner was just arriving. I am lucky that my husband was wise enough to wait until we were outside to question what I was doing. Shortly after we got home, my in-laws called. I dreaded getting on the phone, but I had to let them know I didn't appreciate their doing things to encourage our child to behave in a way that conflicted with what we were trying to teach him. I said if they couldn't support us, then they would have to spend less time with our son.

"I am not a confrontational person, but this was one area I felt strongly needed to be addressed before it grew worse. There were a lot of hurt feelings and tears that night, but as difficult as it was, there were no gray areas left. After that happened, out of the three brothers in my husband's family, we had the easiest relationship with his parents. We didn't get questioned about our parenting but instead were asked about how they should handle situations to be in line with our wishes."

Each family is different, but I hope you're hearing that it's important to think about and nurture this relationship as you go—not wait for an explosion of frustration. My friend Kelly said her mother-in-law seemed overbearing at first. She was a stickler for a Sunday dinner tradition, one that Kelly liked until the exhaustion of parenting made her feel a little resentful for not having a choice on Sunday evenings.

"She loves her son and she loves her grandson, so I had to just pull the positives out. I don't have to cook, and we live near grandparents—grandparents who *want* to be with us," Kelly said. "So even though I'd rather get my son to bed on time, or go to bed myself, I had to say to myself, *This is not a bad thing.*"

Some moms face a different issue—grandparents who prefer to love their grandchildren from a distance and not as frequent babysitters. This can come as a shock if you always assumed your mom or your husband's would be the one to help so you could get a haircut or do lunch with a friend once in a while. You may have even thought your out-of-state parents would be more frequent visitors.

"My kids have certain activities they do with each grandparent that are *unique* and *special* to that relationship. They play cards with Grammy Doreen and Legos with Grandma Donna. I think it's important they have something of their own with each person. They feel *important* and *loved*. It's an anchor for the relationship."

Sheri

The media image of silver-haired, retired grand-parents, who seem not to have a care in the world, is far from my reality. Many of my parents' generation need to keep working and can't retire yet. My own out-of-state parents continue to work in a field they love, and my sisters and I and our kids are not the center of their universe every day. I get that. I respect it. And I swap ideas with other moms on how they bridge the gap creatively between grandparent visits.

Try sliding family pictures into an inexpensive photo album for your kids to play with. Make recognizing names and faces into a game. You can even buy alphabet stickers (P for Papa, for example) to combine love *and* learning. Keep pictures of special people on the refrigerator too.

With some cell phone plans, long-distance calling is much more reasonable than when we were kids. I like to call my folks when one of

What a Trip: Traveling

Perhaps there is nowhere your parenting is more under the microscope than when you are seated with two hundred other people on an airplane, with nowhere to escape, nowhere but a cramped seat where you can feed and console a child. It takes a village to raise a child, but if your child is screaming from his ears popping, the village can be all around you and yet feel very far away.

Here are some ideas aimed at peaceful journeys.

Take extra clothes for both of you in a carry-on. You never know how a flight or the excitement of a trip will affect your child's tummy.

Don't take up luggage space with diapers. Take what you need to get there and buy more at your destination. Always keep a diaper, wipes, and hand sanitizer within reach so you don't have to lug a bag down a slim airplane aisle.

Feed your child on takeoff and landing, or have her pacifier handy. Swallowing helps relieve ear pressure.

Though children can travel on your lap free until age two, consider reserving a seat for your child for long trips, especially if he is busy and mobile. Having him strapped in a car seat on the plane might make for a smoother flight. Ask your airline's policy on half-price tickets for infants or on using an available empty seat.

However long you think it will take you to get somewhere, allow for more time. Being in a stressed-out hurry will make you forget things, and your children pick up on your angst.

with Baby

Take off your kids' shoes. Kicking the seat in front of them is less appealing without the thump.

For children old enough to appreciate it, have a few surprises—toys or snacks—in their bag to be opened only in flight. Once I was advised to take a box of Band-Aids along because children will focus forever on opening Band-Aids and sticking them places.

For babies, think discovery. Bring items that can entertain but that can be lost or discarded without worry—Dixie cups to stack, unstack, and put things in; an old cell phone; a mirrored compact for peek-a-boo.

Always keep a few Ziploc bags handy for separating dirty diapers, icky clothes, a clean pacifier, etc.

Keep smiling. Breathe deeply. Again, your child picks up on your anxiety. Assess the flight attendants early. If you need help, tag the one who made eye contact with or goo-gooed at your child. He or she may have the empathy you need.

Relax and remember, the flight will end, and you probably won't see your fellow passengers ever again!

Explore your airline's website for more information on flying with children. The Federal Aviation Administration offers a printable "Childproof Your Flight" brochure on air safety for little ones. And the site flyingwithkids.com offers extensive and specific advice on just that.

my boys has done something particularly cute. When they were babies, I'd give a call after a checkup at the pediatrician, and now I let my kids dial and say hello, even if their attention span on the phone is only thirty seconds long. Making grandparents part of a regular day, not just a holiday novelty, is important. My parents try to do the same, calling to report to my boys if my dad caught a particularly big fish or to see if my kids are ready to watch an important football game.

If you can afford it, consider giving even modest airline gift certificates for birthday or Christmas presents. You could attach them to a finger painting or handprint, with the caption "Can't wait to hold your hand."

Homemade gifts aren't everyone's cup of tea, but I like the idea of keeping my kids focused on family, on giving, and on creativity. During one visit to my parents' home, my kids were fascinated by a huge bushel of pecans. They played with those nuts for days in every way imaginable. I pocketed about twenty of them. Later I glued them into a shadow box in the shape of a cross, and my oldest son wrote the letters "L-o-v-e y-o-u" on the rest of them and mailed this gift to my parents. The memory of my little nuts' visit will now live on a little longer.

When a grandparent sends your child a gift, always send a prompt thank-you. Involve the kids. We all know how it feels to experience gratitude, and it's a great etiquette lesson to start early with your children.

My children's Nana and Papa started a tradition twenty years ago of recording themselves reading a book and then sending the book and the tape to a grandchild. My nephew would hear their voices and try to tear apart the tape in an attempt to get to them. My oldest son took his afternoon nap for nearly a year by holding a

Thomas the Train book as their voices lulled him to sleep. So priceless! I loved hearing their voices in *his* bedroom.

So often when a family visits grandparents, the newness and energy create an atmosphere that is anything but calm—for kids *or* their parents. As one friend said, "Visiting relatives is just a volcano. Eruptions of family dynamics happen all the time." If it's mom's parents being visited, mom might revert to her behaviors as a daughter, wanting to please, seeking approval. If it's dad's parents, he might do the same, or turn over some parenting responsibility to the open arms of his mom, to the potential dismay of his wife, who could feel she's working overtime trying to parent under the watchful eye of others with more experience.

When you stay under one roof with relatives, your roles of parent, child, and spouse all compete for your attention—and patience. A new mother—or any mother—can feel particularly stressed by the desire to prove herself a good mom.

"You have your self-esteem caught up in your kids' behavior, right or wrong," Kristi said.

Before having kids, visiting family was a vacation for me. When I had kids, I expected the same—a fun change in the routine. But I struggled every time. There were more hands—I had more help—and yet I'd feel unsettled, sometimes unfulfilled at trip's end. And I was prone to bickering with my husband. Eventually I sorted out the feelings I was having. While my husband was able to rest easy with the help of others, I still felt I was working full-time at parenting, which is the way I should have felt; I'm the mom! So my ache for a break collided with my sense of responsibility. And I wanted extended family to think the best of me as a mom, not to think I was handing off my children.

As one friend puts it, "Once I realized going to my in-laws wasn't a vacation, but an extension of what I do at home, I was a lot happier."

Do you crave time at the end of the day when no one needs anything or expects anything of you? On family trips that time dissipates. You have to ask for time alone, for help where you need it. Just remember to take a step back and get perspective, which can be hard to do under someone else's roof but helps you deal with the frustrations.

"I don't think my mother-in-law ever forgave me for taking away her son and then taking him west," Noell said. "It never fails that the day before we leave her house, she picks a fight, maybe so it won't hurt so much to say good-bye. We recognize that now, we expect tension that day, and we accept who she is."

Partnering with your husband is important as you navigate new parental waters. Just as we are to help nurture grandparent-grandchild relationships, a man should encourage a healthy relationship between his wife and his parents, not "play Switzerland" as one friend says of her husband's desire to stay neutral. That said, asking your husband to take sides can be a dangerous thing to do. Strive together to develop respect for the relatives, honesty, and a team approach.

Jamie, who has what she calls a "prickly" relationship with her in-laws, says when she visits them, she always has a close friend on call back home with whom she can vent or process things, so she's not always complaining to her husband. She's called only twice, but she said knowing she has someone "in her corner"—and someone who will offer honest feedback—helps her remember to put a healthy grandparent-grandchild relationship first and get over her own frustrations.

"You accept a lot. You show love a lot. And you take things with a grain of salt," she said.

A final thought on grandparents. Your mother and mother-in-law are two different people. Don't compare them. Don't wish one were more like the other, visited more like the other, gifted more like the other, or loved more like the other. You'd never want them comparing daughters-in-law, would you? Appreciate these women just as they are, as you would have them do for you.

Finding Your Mothering Style
Taking Stock

1. What do I value about my mother and my mother-in-law? What are some concrete ways that I make these women feel their importance in our lives?

2. When family gets involved, what areas of parenting am I most sensitive about?

What do my parents or my in-laws do that I don't like? What are my motives behind wanting to control these aspects of family participation?

3. What dynamics are at work when we travel to see our families? How can we improve on our time spent under their roof?

3

A Discerning Ear

Hearing Your Inner Momma

Perfectionism is the enemy of creation, as extreme self-solitude is the enemy of well-being.

John Updike

I'm not sure how much this Pulitzer Prize–winning writer knows about motherhood, but there aren't truer words spoken about the challenges facing a new mom trying to find her way. We all want to do this job so well, and though the ultimate responsibility for our child lies with us, we can't do it alone.

Advice flows from all directions the moment you announce you are pregnant. It never really stops. One day you too will find yourself offer-

"My mother-in-law told me a great remedy for an ear infection is to blow smoke from a cigarette into the baby's ear. This was not a piece of advice I chose to follow. After taking my son to the ER for croup, she said she didn't think I should give him the prescribed medicines because of the side effects and that humidity would help the most. I wanted to scream, 'I've had him in a steamy bathroom for the last five days!' Instead I said, 'oh, okay.' (I went with the doctor's advice.) You pick your battles. Some things are not worth arguing about."

Terra

ing solutions to problems you haven't been asked to solve. We're all eager to put our hard-earned mommy wisdom to good use.

For now, others are likely the teachers, and you are the student. Each day your insights, your intuition, and your knowledge grow—if you listen to others as well as yourself.

When Kelly's son was three months old, he was sleeping in her bed at night. Her mother-in-law was disapproving and direct: "He's going to bring home a girlfriend one day and still be sleeping in your room," she pronounced.

A weary Kelly took a breath. She told her mother-in-law it was the only thing that had worked to keep the baby from crying all night. She agreed it was a habit in need of breaking. Then Kelly said four very important words: "I don't know how."

That evening, Grandma told her son to take his tired wife out for ice cream. As they were enjoying

"I think the decision to stay at home or go back to work was the most controversial one I encountered. The opinions were everywhere. I was working full-time when I adopted Daniel, and I knew that I would want to be home with him full-time. I think moms who stay home have a lot of bad information about moms who work and vice versa. Women have to make the choice that is right for them. I can't know what is guiding others' decisions, just as they can't know what guides mine."

Dana

a treat, the truth came out. Grandma was putting the baby to bed in his crib.

After that night the infant never returned to mom's bed.

"It's hard to admit you need help," Kelly said. "He cried again, but I knew I could work it out because he'd slept in his crib. That was huge."

You might feel a little overwhelmed as a new mom. Have you read all the books on child care but are still unsure of yourself? Does conflicting advice confuse you? That's all a normal part of finding your way.

There are certain truths that you can rely on. For example, if you are dealing with a medical issue, perhaps a fever that worries you, always consult your pediatrician. Even if a dozen moms tell you that your baby's fever doesn't meet the threshold for a doctor visit, even if you see similar advice in a trustworthy book like the American Academy of Pediatrics' *Caring for Your*

Baby and Young Child: Birth to Age Five, if you are concerned, call the doctor. Often a nurse on the phone can help you sort out whether a visit is necessary. But trust your gut. Someday you will likely be one of those moms who is comfortable monitoring an unexplained fever at home, but for now you are learning.

There's a difference between getting advice from other moms and being judged by them. Advice is well-meaning. When you receive opinions and suggestions, how do you feel? Receptive, threatened, overwhelmed, thankful, annoyed, competitive? Assess your reaction. Try to figure out why you feel that way and you may open your mind a little wider. You should, because the best suggestions you will hear in mothering will come from other moms. So will some of the worst, and the source of both might even be the same person. You'll have to be discerning.

"When children are young and you are a new mom, you think that your child should be doing exactly what every other child is doing. But the development of children early on is so varied. I still have to remember that just because my children are not doing something—or are doing more than other children their age—it doesn't mean they are less smart or smarter than others. It just means they are as unique as God planned them to be. His plan is greater than the timing of when they learn to sit, walk, talk, jump, or read. He is in charge, not me."

Tracy

Couldn't Live without It

Some tools of the trade moms call indispensable—
and wish they'd found sooner

A sound machine: It produces noises—like rain, wind, or a heartbeat—that soothe baby and muffle other noises around the house. Some are as small as a paperback book—easy to bring along when you travel.

The heat buddy: A large, soft, fan-shaped pad you warm in the microwave to bring comfort to engorged breasts and aching muscles.

Kipiis: A clip that turns any napkin or paper towel into a bib.

Gas drops and the leg bicycle: Baby's tummy bubbles seem to be popped—or at the very least the baby is distracted—by a drop of simethicone on his tongue. Pumping those legs, with baby's bottom raised slightly, can also work out gas cramps.

Wet wipes: Keep them in every room of the house and on every row of seats of every vehicle the family owns.

The SwaddleMe blanket: Also called a Miracle Blanket, it allows even the most folding-challenged parent to wrap baby into a comforting cocoon.

A breast pump: It gives you the ability to nurse and yet share with your husband the wonder of nourishing a newborn.

Disposable bibs: These are especially good for travel. They are not environmentally friendly, but finding a crusty bib in your diaper bag is a drag.

Diaper backpacks: Men seem more comfortable carrying the goods this way, and backpacks free your arms from a tote bag that often slides off your shoulder.

The Pack 'n Play: One mom calls it "a familiar container," which, if you get your child used to it early, can expand your ability to spend time with other people while your baby naps. It's also a great corral for crawlers while you make dinner or tackle a project that demands some focus.

"My first playgroup was obsessed with every aspect of parenting, and that was stressful. We compared everything. If my child wasn't similar to others, I would worry. I finally decided to accept and appreciate Jacob's individuality. I enjoyed mothering more. I tried to go with my instincts, trust what felt right, and pray when I didn't know what to do."

Sheri

My grandmother, who raised four daughters in an era lacking five-point-harness car seats, breast pumps, and disposable diapers, gave me a tiny spiral notebook at my baby shower to jot down memories or advice. She wrote on the first page: "Always look in your baby's eyes when you speak to him. It matters." What an awesome insight! She also said, often, that children should be seen and not heard. I respectfully disagree.

Be gracious when other people grandstand. Remember these moms when you start dispensing your own opinions. Certain topics polarize moms: pacifiers, co-sleeping, working mothers, how early to start anything from solid food to preschool. How can you opine on an issue if you don't *consider the child*? Some children need solid food at five months; others can wait till eight months. Every child is different. Use that as your shield against anyone who might otherwise make you feel inferior. We all make parenting mistakes. We

"The best thing I ever did was to decide what I thought was best using common sense. Then I used my pediatrician as a sounding board and formulated a baseline for what I thought to be best. By not being a 'clean slate,' with nothing but room for others to write on, I was able to have productive, two-sided conversations when talking with other mothers. Suggestions came in the form of casual conversations rather than 'You know what you ought to do' statements. Then I was able to tweak that 'baseline' according to what I liked or didn't from what I'd learned from talking to others."

Kim

all keep striving to do our best. And we all know our own child better than anyone else on earth.

One mom tells a story of being swayed from her "inner momma." A friend wanted to do her a favor by picking up her children from a nature class their kids shared. The boys heard the woman's offer and cried, "No, no!"

"She got in my face and said, 'You know you're enabling them, don't you? They will never be able to separate from you when they get to school. They will probably live with you until they are forty.' Somehow she talked me into letting her pick them up."

Angry with herself for backtracking under pressure, the mom ended up picking up her children anyway, enduring more pointed comments. But walking home on a beautiful day, her clouds of self-doubt began to dissipate.

"Initially, I was angry. But I know my boys. I know they don't have trouble separating," she

10 COMMANDMENTS for Mothers in 1918

When baby advice seems overflowing and overwhelming, consider what women nearly one hundred years ago were being told. You'll see that some advice is solid through time, while other words of wisdom don't seem so wise as they age. This is something to remember as you get and give your share of suggestions.

I. Never give drugs other than those prescribed by the doctor to your baby. It may mean his death.

II. Never give Baby a taste of this food and that food until he is well out of babyhood.

III. Always give Baby a bath at the same time every day and be sure that the water is not over 98 degrees and that he is never left for a moment alone.

IV. Never allow anyone to kiss Baby near his mouth or on his hand. You can save him many colds and illnesses.

V. Never put Baby to bed until he has had a good bowel movement.

VI. Keep Baby out of doors at least an hour each clear day, and in mild weather several hours each day.

VII. Give Baby a bed to himself and, if possible, a room to himself.

VIII. Consult your doctor whenever in doubt. A small consultation fee frequently saves a large doctor's bill.

IX. Read everything about babies that you can get; send to the Children's Bureau at Washington for bulletins concerning care of babies; do everything in your power to educate yourself for motherhood.

X. Use your common sense, plenty of soap and water, and an abundance of good medical advice.

From *A Book for Mothers* (Earnshaw Knitting Co., 1918)

said. "I have to respect and listen to my kids. I trust their instincts and I need to trust my own maternal instincts. It's hard if you've been raised as a pleaser."

As you raise your child and start to make a multitude of daily choices, be aware that sometimes a one-time decision starts a pattern you aren't expecting. I can't remember how my first son developed the habit of wearing socks on his hands to sleep. He just said he felt safer that way. Cute, right? We even took pictures. When he started wanting the socks to cover his elbows, I wondered briefly if I was aiding an obsessive-compulsive child. It was charming, not harming, though it did go on for the better part of six months.

Some call these things quirks; others say they are props—something a child comes to need to sleep or eat or be content. I have a neighbor whose daughter sleeps with a dozen or so pacifiers—in

"I have found myself in slight verbal altercations with family and friends with regard to disciplining my son. I try very hard now not to discipline anyone's children but my own. It just drives me crazy when other people try to correct or punish my kid, especially without explanation or with an impatient, angry voice. When you as a parent are working on something at home like sharing, manners, or not throwing toys, you want to *encourage* your child, as well as correct him."

Lisa

her hands, on her chest, sprinkled in the crib around her. Another friend had a son who insisted on wearing Batman pajamas at all times—all times—for several months. Endearing? I thought so. Wasn't my child.

But there's another level of props that experienced moms will tell you to beware of, like rocking or nursing your baby to sleep. I'm the first to say having a baby fall asleep in your arms is a beautiful thing. Savor those precious moments. Just be aware that what may seem like a working situation for a week may not feel so good a year later. Introducing a comfort object early on, like a blankie or a musical animal, can be a great signal that it's time to go to bed but still train your child to get to sleep on her own. Just be sure you don't lose that blankie or animal! The point is, trust yourself but resist bad habits.

"My sister-in-law nurses her baby to sleep for every nap, and I just get frustrated because it

"My daughter was outgrowing her bassinette, but she didn't like the crib at all. My sister-in-law suggested I hang my clothes over the side to see if being able to smell me would comfort her. I used a polka-dotted nightgown one day. It became Hanna's favorite 'blanket.' For a while it was whole, but then we lost it at a restaurant and went back to find it in the parking lot under the tire of a car, so my husband had to rip it out. I cut it into a few pieces at that point so we'd always have another. There aren't many polka dots left on it these days. She's seven now."

Sara

interrupts and hampers group plans," one mom said. "Everyone agrees the baby is not getting enough healthy sleep, and she complains about her own exhaustion because her daughter never sleeps more than ten minutes. It's hard to know how to help without intruding. You just want the best for the mom and the child."

When you experience parenting success, whether it's an infant's sleep pattern or a toddler's potty training or a third grader's math mastery, it's natural to want to share your insights. Always remember what it's like to be on the receiving end of information. Praise a mom for her efforts. Suggest but don't preach. Keep your sense of humor, and, when you see the opportunity, help another mom keep hers. You may be just the strand of sanity she needs at that moment.

"You want to be so perfect and do all that those books say—and then you want to burn them," Angela said. "I finally realized what I wanted was excellence not perfection. There is no perfection."

My friend Noell advises new moms: "It took ten years for me to stop relying on other people to give me a report card for how I was doing as a mom. Do yourself a favor—don't wait that long."

Finding Your Mothering Style
Taking Stock

1. What's been my most memorable mom-moment so far? What emotion did that prompt in me?

2. Do I trust myself as a mom? Why or why not? Are there steps I could take to gain confidence?

3. How am I at taking advice or suggestions on my mothering?

4. What have I already learned that I would pass along to a new mom or mom-to-be?

5. Have my husband and I started anything with our baby that is destined to become a habit? How do we each feel about that?

Friends

Finding Companionship and
Support in Other Mothers

I recall sitting at my desk at work, pregnant, amazed by my inability to concentrate. I wanted to surf the Web to find out what was happening in my womb at a given week. I would daydream and doodle name possibilities. My belly was the new center of my universe. I felt bathed in a spotlight of newness that no one else seemed to appreciate. I had a co-worker who didn't even realize that I'd gone on maternity leave. She just wasn't in the childbearing phase of her own life and didn't realize that thirty-eight weeks pregnant meant time to deliver.

When our bodies and minds change that much, our relationships do the same. Old friends bump

"It can be *tough* when your old friends don't understand how a baby can **consume your every** thought. They are still going out for happy hour. Your happy hour is now a good feeding or long naptime."

Angela

into your new priorities. Some roll with it; some do not.

I had grand visions of returning to my workplace for a visit, my darling little newborn in tow. I expected attention, conversation, congratulations. I got some of that, briefly. But as I was leaving, I stopped and turned around and was stunned at how the place where my son and I had been standing was now swallowed up by a strategy meeting. It was like I'd never even been there.

"I think it's just you and me, kid," I said to a pair of big blue eyes.

Historically, I have hated endings. Graduations, departures, even Christmas nights have left me feeling incredibly empty. Friendships don't usually stop on a dime, but even their gradual dwindling can make me sad, even if there's something or someone else delightful right around the corner.

Single friends, childless couples, even those trying to have children are in a different place than you are now. With effort and understanding—and common interests—those friendships can stand the test of time and change. Imagine a single woman, yearning to find the man she can share her life with, hearing a new mom go on and on about her baby's long nights. If you were aching for a family of your own, chances are you might not be too empathetic. It's enriching to everyone involved to connect with friends in another phase of life. What great perspective, and a great reminder, that it's not all about you! And if one day your single friends have children, imagine what a knowledgeable support you can be.

I'm convinced true friendship is vital during the early years of motherhood. Your learning curve is enormous, and so too can be your sense of isolation. In the past, school and work provided an automatic pool of people with whom you could connect. Now you're "home alone" but hungry to share the journey with other women.

"I wanted **friends** so **badly** when we moved to the mountains. But with no sidewalks, and neighbors in their retirement years, I found out quickly I had to go to the people. For me what fit was the public library's weekly story time. **Reading brings moms together.** I listened intently and found out more information about my community the first three weeks of attending story time than in any other venue. While I didn't feel comfortable enough to attend **playgroups** at first, I found myself listening intently to the conversations of other moms and giving out my personal info—email, address, etc.—to be included on information exchanges."

Lisa

So where do you find friends? Oddly enough, I found my first mom friends in a grief group. There were four of us who had suffered the loss of a baby and had attended a couples' course to help us cope with our losses. We each went on to get pregnant in the next year or so, and with those celebrated little miracles, we started getting together every couple of weeks. We went to the zoo together, the museum, and many, many parks. We spent a lot of time in each other's living rooms, watching those kids grow into toddlers and beyond.

You can meet moms in tumbling classes for little ones when your kids can't even roll over yet, the pool, the library, sign language classes, the gym, the pediatrician's office, church, the aisles of a baby megastore, and the crown jewel of many childhoods, the park. Keep a notepad handy in your purse to jot down names and numbers. In this Internet age many women can type "playgroup"

"The first six weeks you are trying to figure out which way is up. I wasn't getting the warm, snuggly mommy feeling instantly. What saved my life was a 'Help, I Have a Newborn!' class I signed up for through the hospital. There were ten or eleven of us with new babies and a nurse who held our hands and walked us through everything— even how to go out to dinner with a baby. When the six-week class was over, we thought, *We can't not have a place to go on Wednesday mornings.* So we formed a little playgroup."

Susan

Play

Make no mistake, playgroups are not always calm affairs! They begin as sweet baby-watching sessions, but as the kids get busier, more mobile, and more messy with a snack, sometimes such gatherings feel like organized chaos. Rest assured, friends and memories last much longer than any mess. Here are some thoughts on productive playgroups.

Who: It's helpful to have something in common: children the same ages, same neighborhood, same church, and so on. But open your mind and heart to others. You may want to limit your group to about six children. Too many people might overwhelm your child and undermine your goal of connecting in a real way with other moms. If you create a playgroup of children who live fairly close, they can continue to connect as friends on their own later.

What: If you are starting from scratch, talk with the other moms about what you'd like your group to be. Discuss guidelines for siblings attending, sick children, inappropriate behavior, cancellation, and inclement weather. Some groups are very laid-back, while others find success in structure.

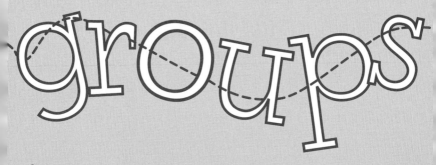

groups

Where: Trade houses or try new parks. Meet to walk the mall, picnic at the zoo, try the baby pool, or explore a pumpkin patch. Alternate adventures with home meetings, so the process of getting to know each other isn't overshadowed by activities. Create a roster that includes cell phone numbers—great to have when someone runs late or you are trying to find each other at a new venue.

When: Midmorning seems to work best for kids and moms alike, but have the foresight to change times if tardiness is a problem or too many naps and feedings seem to be thrown off. Consider whether monthly, biweekly, or weekly fits your schedules and your needs.

Why: The purposes of a playgroup should be to give each other a lift, share advice, and engage your children in fun play. Stay away from competition, gossip, and unnecessary drama.

How: Rotate hostesses so someone is a point person for each gathering. Be committed if you join, so you don't take a spot that another mom might truly need!

and the name of their city and come up with a place to start meeting other moms.

My friend Sara took a prenatal/postnatal exercise class when she was pregnant. She chatted up a few women she thought she'd never see again. When she returned with her newborn daughter for another class, she caught up with one mom-to-be from her previous class. They clicked, and much of the class became trusted friends. Together they started a playgroup. Seven years and seven more births later, the playgroup the women started remains connected.

You never know to whom you're talking, whether in a formal setting like a class or casually in a grocery store line. It could be someone you need in your life, or someone who needs you. Don't give up too early on people or activities.

If you are an introvert, it may be difficult to get out as a new mom, let alone strike up conversations with strangers. Structured classes may help

"I met a mom who was a *friend* of a friend. We began to switch kids weekly for three hours to get a little *time* for ourselves, and we'd walk with the strollers three mornings a week. When I was working so much, it was easy to make excuses for not attending Bible study. She challenged my *faith* and helped me *grow*. That was huge."

Kris

you there. Remember, it only takes a small step to get a conversation rolling.

> "I love your daughter's shoes. Where did you find those?"
> "Are you happy with that stroller?"
> "It's nice to get out, isn't it?"

Don't forget neighbors. We were childless and pretty unconnected for years in our neighborhood—garage door up, garage door down at the end of the workday. We didn't even know for weeks that a neighbor two houses down had given birth five days before I did. Having children changed everything. Nearby mom friends are a unique blessing. Walk your neighborhood. You may be surprised at the number of women doing the same.

When you meet women whom you feel a connection to, take the next step and grow that connection. Our group of friends and babies from that

"As a competitive person, it was very hard for me not to **compare my children** to other people's children. When I started a playgroup, Ben's development lagged behind the other boys. He had trouble communicating, which also made him more unruly than the other children. Honestly, it would make me mad at Ben that he couldn't be like the other boys. Of course I never actually said anything to Ben—he was only about eighteen months old—but I would find myself short-tempered after these playdates. **I remember the moms asking if I was worried about him** or if I thought about getting him tested. I think it made them feel good about their own children to make me worry about mine. Then I really worried about Ben's speech for the next year and a half until he started preschool when his teachers assured me that he was fine and **I had nothing to worry about.**"

Tracy

grief group became known as "the lunch bunch." We met on Wednesdays at one of our homes, and whoever hosted got the pleasure of a few hours out by herself, while the rest of us caught up and kept up with the kids. And of course, we lunched.

Playgroups, and the more intimate *playdates*, are popular and useful. Women get to connect; babies start to socialize. The information exchange and support can be awesome, as is exposing kids to sharing and to other loving adults. It's also very helpful for your child to learn to nap out of her own crib.

Playgroup dynamics are as varied as the children they gather. Give yourself time to settle in. Give a new group time to find its rhythm, and then assess how it's working for you. Do you look forward to the fellowship? Do you get nervous about your child's behavior? Do you dread the constant comparisons or gossipy atmosphere? Answering such questions about your experience

"I have noticed it takes a lot of **trust** on my part to allow somebody new into my life. My favorite **friendships** are the ones where both of us take risks to share deep parts of ourselves and each of us is mature enough to handle it. That's what makes a friendship trustworthy and **long-lasting.**"

Tracy

with the playgroup will help you decide if it's right for you.

A friend told me she read about a playgroup in which a woman sharply criticized moms who choose not to breast-feed—as she poured diet soda into her children's sippy cups. Sounds a little extreme, but you get the picture. Follow your values. Follow your heart. Keep your personal priorities intact.

In Terra's first playgroup, she was surrounded by other moms who were fellow therapists and teachers. "I always saw competitiveness between moms regarding whose child sat up first, crawled first, walked first," she said. "One of my friends wouldn't go to playgroup if a certain mother hosted, because she felt like her son was a bully and bad influence.

"You see the same things as your children grow up. I've had parents ask me how my daughter did on her report card. These situations make me think that people are not very confident in their own parenting styles and in their children. It's okay that kids develop differently and have different strengths and weaknesses. It's just not always necessary to point them out to other moms."

Personally, nothing alienates me from a playgroup or any group of women quicker than gossip, whether it's about other moms and other kids, or especially if it's related to male bashing and disrespecting marriage. It's great to have an outlet other than your husband, but friends shouldn't become an outlet for your talking negatively *about* your husband. Another note on dads: it's wonderful if you can connect with mom friends as full families once in a while, so dad can feel more a part of your daytime world and maybe meet a guy *he'd* like to spend more time with. What a treasure it is to have a whole family your whole family enjoys spending time with!

Less Time, Same Need
FINDING MOM FRIENDS WHEN YOU WORK

Creating a network of mom friends can be a bit more challenging when you work. You can still take classes, go to the park, rely on your neighborhood, but the reality is that your time for doing so is much more limited. Here are some thoughts from working moms on ways they met and maintained relationships as they went back to the workplace.

Keep an open mind. Terra was at a work Christmas party when she was invited to join a playgroup. Karen kicked off a great relationship with another working mom when their kids started babbling to each other in a scrapbook store one Saturday.

Don't put off meeting other moms. "I worked with my first child and then quit before my second," Mary said. "But I feel like everybody's already got their groups. I wish I had tried sooner."

Consider attending new mom classes at the hospital. They can attract other working moms who are still on maternity leave.

See your co-workers in a new light, whatever stage of parenting they may be in. You might find a new friend in an experienced mom who you didn't connect with before you were a mom.

Consider joining a local chapter of Mothers of Preschoolers (MOPS.org) or the La Leche League (llli.org) that meets in the evenings.

Attend a weekend story time at the public library.

Consider online support groups. "I remember going through periods of devastating loneliness," Ellen said of her days as a new mom and a full-time senior systems engineer. "Online groups helped because they were a way to connect with moms like me that didn't involve having to get my kids packed up and out of the house, go somewhere, spend energy and possibly money I didn't have. I could get online from home while the kids were sleeping. They were a great social outlet as well as excellent for information and ideas." You can chat online or search for a playgroup to attend in person in your town.

Network through stay-at-home moms. Ask them about their working mom friends. Also consider the possibility of a trusted friend who doesn't work as a source of child care. Some stay-at-home moms would welcome the chance to earn money by caring for your child, and you might rest easier knowing your child was in the hands of a friend. A win-win situation for all concerned.

Make the most of Sunday mornings. If you attend church, your child's Sunday school class or a young families class are great places to connect with other parents. If forming a Saturday playgroup sounds appealing, ask your church about posting a notice for interested moms.

Having friends who share your parenting style and values becomes more and more important as children get older. First, your time becomes even more precious as your family grows. You simply have less of it to dedicate to friends. Also, discipline may well become a regular feature of your time together, as children test you, as is their job. It's helpful if those with whom you spend time have similar expectations and limits. As you mature as a mom, you will develop a clearer sense of yourself as a parent and a woman. You will know which friends uplift you and your children and which do not.

Finding mom friends is survival. Being one is just as important. You've seen the woman in the grocery store, the one with the screaming child and a full cart. Did you wince? In your mind did you criticize her lack of control? Did you offer encouragement? I think we each have a responsibility to this sisterhood of mothers. At some point, you will be "that woman." How would you want to be treated?

Once I was at a park, chatting with a friend, and another mom was playing with her toddler very nearby. We were in the same general area for an hour before the woman got up the courage to ask me about the church we'd been discussing. She was days new to Colorado, a house full of boxes and a heart full of uncertainty, and here she was prioritizing her child with a picnic and monkey bars. I showered her with information about pediatricians, hair salons, schools, and more parks. I really hope I brightened her day just a tad. She reminded me that you never know where the mom next to you is coming from.

My first playgroup ended gradually, with geography, school schedules, and different lifestyles all coming into play. I still love each woman who was in the group. That we don't meet regularly anymore doesn't diminish what we had or how we helped each other through a formative period in our lives as women and mothers. Change will happen, and we have to let it, whether with our kids or our friends.

Finding Your Mothering Style
Taking Stock

1. How have I seen my relationships change since becoming a mother?

2. Where did many of my current friendships start? What do I value in a girlfriend?

3. What kind of a friend am I? In what ways would I like to improve?

4. In what kinds of settings am I most comfortable meeting people? Am I more social

butterfly or hermit crab? How would I like to grow in the area of making friends?

5. What activities appeal to me when it comes to meeting other moms?

5

Keeping Perspective

The Woman behind the Mother

As you cultivate your parenting style and your new community, it's important to remember the *you* beyond the youngsters. There are plenty of pastimes that may have to wait for less busy times, but it's important to find some time for yourself in this era when selflessness is so often required.

My friend Angela went through a time when she felt busy as a mother but lost as a woman. "I realized I didn't have to give all of me up. I had to step back and say just because I'm not working doesn't mean I have to let go of everything I was," she said. "You just have to find new

"Never doubt that a COMMUNITY of thoughtful, committed women, filled with the power and love of God, using gifts they have identified and developed, and pouring passions planted in them by God—never doubt that these women can change the world."

Lynne Hybels, *Nice Girls Don't Change the World*

niches and support groups that validate what you're doing."

In the early days of mothering, my book group was my special niche. Finishing a novel gave me a rush. Being with women who respected my role as a mom but wanted to talk about much more was very grounding and humbling.

"I still have dreams and desires and aspirations other than motherhood," Barb says. "I feel deprived when those can't move forward as quickly as I'd like. I didn't have the *aha*! moment of finding the perfect career, that thing that propels you before you have kids. So I try to do small things to keep learning and growing."

My friend Sara's mom started an interior decorating business, sewing drapes at home when Sara was young, and later setting up a studio in the basement. Her entrepreneurial spirit, combined with her family-first mantra, was so inbred in Sara that she's done the same, opening a scrapbooking

"I have been a self-starter,
a *dreamer*—
motivated my whole life.
But some of that evaporated
in the years after having kids.
I knew my husband's and
my children's needs, dreams, and desires
better than I knew my own.
I was helping them to pursue these things
while neglecting myself.
I began, on some level,
to adopt their dreams as my own.
Simple indulgences can be
satisfying yet hollow, while
passion-filled pursuits
can bring wholeness and honor
over the long haul. It's a process,
an awakening, after you have kids."

Kim

retreat house that allows her to be home with her school-age daughters and husband throughout the week and pursue a business and a passion many weekends.

Some moms just want the opportunity to talk politics, to feel valued as an individual with thoughts and opinions, or to simply spend a day unslimed by a little person. If this is you, you aren't alone. Find a partner and stimulate those brain cells beyond Elmo. Have a grown-up meal with a friend. If you don't desire those things, consider why. It's worth the effort to connect with your God-given dreams because what you have to offer matters profoundly to your family and your community and continues as your children grow. Your goal, after all, is to work yourself out of a job.

I worked so hard at becoming a mom that I was quite content with my new role. I was proud of it and didn't seek a periodic escape like some

"I popped in a CD of all my downloaded business school documents from when I was getting my MBA. I was looking for a marketing plan that I had remembered developing that I thought my husband could possibly utilize with his new business. As I was reading it, I thought, *Oh my gosh, I did this. I really am smart!* Then I sat and thought how disconnected I felt with who I was then. But as I started to get depressed, I looked at my two-month-old sleeping and popped in on my three-year-old snoring away and I quickly realized I wouldn't trade any of this diaper-changing business for that. I want to use my degree again, but watching Preston giggle yesterday was more exciting than reading that old marketing plan. It's so important for mothers to keep in tune with the fact that they are women too and to keep in tune with what makes them happy when they aren't fussing over their children. You must do something for yourself."

Kelly

of my friends. The escapist needs came only after three kids, like my penchant for coffee did. Over the years I've come to see motherhood as not *de*fining me but *re*fining me. This insight is key to preserving your identity in these early years. You are still who you were before children, but the process of parenting can make you a better woman.

For some women, the thing they do for themselves is simply to do less. "Over time I have come to realize my relationships with other women are far more important to me than a clean house, so sometimes they are invited to join me in my messy house," Julie said.

"Thinning out my schedule was hard for me to do," she added. "When I tell people the limited things I am involved with, I often get a funny look of disapproval. But it always comes back to 'What is *my* end result?' Now I feel like I can give my best to what I am involved with instead of being

Reconnecting

Consider your passions, pre-children and now that you are a mom. Do you wish you were still jogging? Still a movie buff? Still interested in that cause overseas? Are there creative ways to pursue those things as a mom?

Read a book not related to child-rearing. Even if it takes two months, the satisfaction and stimulation will still be rewarding.

Try something new. A recipe, an exercise class, a new way to arrange your living room. Renewal is refreshing.

Consider waking up in time to do something for yourself before the children rise. It might be more rewarding than the extra half hour of sleep.

Journal. Having an outlet for your ideas and dreams is important, even when day-to-day life may hinder them for a while.

Have a discussion with your husband about what he thinks your gifts or strengths are. Are you using them? You might be surprised by the support you get for non-mom activities.

Assess your use of time. When you have an hour, are you watching brainless TV? Are you always cleaning? Perhaps you are preventing yourself from having the time to recognize the woman behind the mom.

with You

involved in many things and really not doing my best. I have learned that saying no is one of the hardest things for me to do, yet I am rewarded every time I find the courage to do so." Your new village—friends or family members—can help you sort through these feelings. Ask a veteran mom, maybe someone whose kids have flown the nest, how she preserved the woman inside the mother—maybe even what she would have done differently. You'll be valuing her mothering experience as she helps you plot yours. That's what the village is all about.

Finding Your Mothering Style
Taking Stock

1. Beyond my child, what are my passions and my goals? Is there something I can do in this busy season to further them?

"I've known moms that can't separate their kids' actions from their own. They take ownership of a fussy day or they apologize for a cranky toddler like they are responsible for his teething. You put undue pressure on your kids and yourself when you do that. Your children don't define you."

Stephanie

2. What is something new I'd like to try?

3. Do I consider myself a leader or a follower? What qualities in myself would I like to work on?

6

Sitter Savvy

Finding Child Care You Trust

An important aspect of cultivating your new community as a mom is identifying a group of people to whom you can entrust those precious children when you need to be away.

During much of my adolescence, I babysat. I loved the kids, loved the independence and trust I felt, and loved the income. But when it came to getting a sitter for my own kids, I didn't do it. For five years I didn't. I was lucky enough to have my in-laws and a sister living nearby who were willing to babysit, so they were essential to making my extracurricular plans possible.

I was fortunate but silly. As our obligations and desires for grown-up time grew and our need for child care increased beyond what felt comfortable to ask of family, it came time to find a sitter. I was paralyzed by apprehension. Now I had three children under six, including a baby. I'd missed the window for having a teen sitter grow with my kids, and I had forgotten the trust that was once invested in me as a babysitter.

If I had followed the advice I now hear from other moms, I would have been able to hire a babysitter without stressing over the idea so much.

Setting Up a Sitter Network

Cultivate sitters early. Get to know kids who are approaching babysitting age, so they can get to know your children.

Ask your friends for referrals of good babysitters. Sometimes moms are possessive of a favorite babysitter, and who can blame them? But referrals are everything.

If you live near a university, consider college students, especially those pursuing a field connected to children. My sister-in-law interviewed college kids, and the one she chose babysat just about every Saturday night for eleven years and even accompanied them occasionally on vacations. They attended her wedding and eventually celebrated the birth of her kids!

Consider Sunday school teachers or volunteers, or even preschool teachers as possible sitters, knowing the church or school has already established a level of trust with them.

Interview your sitter over the phone. If you are impressed by the interview, arrange a meeting in your home. Watch how she or he interacts with your children.

Check references. Always talk to a mom who has used the sitter, asking about punctuality, how

Good to Go?

It's OK to leave your kids. You'd probably tell any friend or stranger that. You'd mean it wholeheartedly. So why is it so hard to let that advice soak in when it's *you* leaving *your* kids?

I could interview a thousand different moms and hear a thousand different stories about how it feels to leave your child in the hands of another. Yours would be different still. As for me, I felt a fair amount of guilt early on. I could be attending a meeting at church, getting my hair highlighted, or going to dinner with my husband—all good causes—and I'd still somehow feel a little "wrong" for leaving my kids with someone else. *Was I too connected to them, too controlling? Did I trust others too little? Did I have a warped sense of how much they needed me—or what I deserved to do outside the home? Did I think I was failing as a mom if I needed time away?* I've come to see I was, and am, pretty normal in my hesitancy to leave.

Guilt is unproductive. I eventually reasoned that you cannot and should not go your child's entire life without leaving them in someone else's hands. So if it had to happen, I wasn't going to make myself miserable each time. I made sure I kept talking to friends who were familiar with the sitter routine and would comfort me or call me silly in proportion to my worries. I was also particular about who kept my kids, so that when I departed I was confident I had done my homework and left my children and their caregiver as prepared as possible.

Also, spelling out to myself what I was doing helped me gain perspective. Was I leaving to indulge in some bad habit? Was I wasting money? Was I seeking to run away from something, like a colicky baby, or running toward something, like a change of scenery or some couple time? It wasn't about right or wrong reasons, but about being thoughtful instead of emotional.

I have several friends who don't think twice about using sitters and grabbing time to sit at a coffee shop alone. I know some feel guilty that they *don't* feel guilty about leaving! The same exercise in thinking through what you are doing can help put these feelings in proper perspective too.

I realized pretty quickly as a new mom that my baby would pick up on that anxiety. And so do toddlers on up. If I was excited about what I was leaving to do, and the trustworthy person I was leaving them with, there was a chance they would be too. If I cried upon departing, there was a *very* good chance they would too. I felt I had to rein in my uncertainty for their sakes.

It's healthy for a child to learn to listen to and feel comfortable with other adults. It's great for children to learn mommies have needs too. It may be hard to tell yourself these things with a child crying and clinging to your leg as you try to make it out the door. Is there a worse feeling? But there's another reason to go. Your child will eventually be left at school, or a church nursery, and the sooner they learn that they are safe, and that you will return, the sooner you can enjoy successful and maybe even cheerful farewells.

he or she handles stress and discipline issues, and how the kids felt about the person.

Don't always judge a sitter by his or her age. Many moms find preteens to be more conscientious, have fewer distractions, and express more genuine interest in their kids than do high schoolers. Always speak to the parents of any minor you are considering hiring, and ask their opinion of their child's level of responsibility.

Ask your sitter to take an American Red Cross Babysitter's Training Course and become CPR certified. Visit redcross.org for more information and classes in your area.

Try out your sitter for a short time during the day, or even while you stay at home. Consider popping in to see how things are going when you aren't expected.

Ask your children (if they can tell you) how the time went, what they liked, what they played, and what they ate. You never know. One sitter fed my friend's daughter Popsicles and crackers for dinner. She couldn't work the microwave. Also inquire whether the sitter spent time on the phone or computer.

Treat sitters with respect. Have a snack they like and pay them well. Be clear about your expectations. What is intuitive to you might not be to a teenager.

Extend that respect to payment. Ask other moms the going rate and make sure you are clear with your sitter on what you pay.

Don't automatically assume that just because you trust your sitter, you can also trust your sitter's friend. Your sitter's opinion counts, but you still need to check out the friend before hiring him or her to babysit. You may want to use a team to do the babysitting job. A team has its advantages—more eyes and ears and hands—but if they are more interested

"We went to the local community college and posted an ad at the student center and in the education department with our specifications. This worked wonderfully with us considering most students' flexibility. Another wonderful resource can be the local churches. We have found wonderful babysitters for evenings and summer by asking the girls I volunteer with on Sunday mornings. Most churches do a background check and fingerprint prior to allowing anyone to volunteer, so there is peace of mind that they are prescreened."

Stephanie

in each other than the kids, the team will just be a distraction.

Consider swapping children with trusted friends. It's cheaper than hiring a sitter and can lessen your anxiety.

So whom did *I* find? A friend who knew I was looking for a sitter told me there was an awesome preteen girl who worked in her church nursery. She was so impressed with the girl she started delving deeper on my behalf. Turns out, and this is no joke, she lived on my street. Her mother is a teacher, her father a firefighter. *On my street!* She's the kind of kid who spontaneously creates a volleyball camp for the neighborhood boys and looks out for them whether she's on the clock or not. What a treasure! I only wish I'd found her sooner.

So of course my favorite advice is to look out your window. Know those neighbors. Having a sitter you don't have to transport is not only nice but essential when your husband is out of town and the kids are in bed when you get home from your evening out.

Personally, I'm also a big fan of the family sitting swap. You watch ours; we'll watch yours. I think it's good for dads to see what it takes to take on other children for the sake of safe, reciprocal babysitting. It's cheaper, and your kids get to nurture friendships, you nurture couple friendships, and you help other couples and yourselves nurture your marriages.

However you do it, your "new village" has to include a sitter or two, for sanity's sake.

Finding Your Mothering Style
Taking Stock

1. How do I feel about leaving my child with a babysitter? Do I have a plan for doing so?

"I just love the idea of a babysitting co-op, and it saves me a ton of money. You have to be recommended by a current member, then have your house inspected for safety by one of the officers of the co-op. You pay $30 for coupons and use them to 'pay' other members to watch your kiddos. You earn them back by watching other kids in the co-op. The group members each have two to four children and you earn more 'coupons' the more children you agree to watch. I feel so comfortable with sitters knowing they are other moms who are depending on me too."

Elizabeth

2. Does needing time away make me feel like I'm somehow less of a good mom? If so, how can I gain perspective?

3. Do I have a friend or family member I can trust with whom I can trade babysitting? Is there a family that might consider swapping with us on a regular basis?

4. What qualities do my husband and I feel are essential in a sitter? How can I determine if an applicant has these qualities?

The Bottom Line

Staying True to You

I usually attempt to create a Christmas card featuring a photo of my boys. One year I tried several times to get the right picture. First, it was my three boys in handsome sweaters at a community outing. Then they were in Christmas pajamas near our tree. Then they posed at my in-laws' house. I even attempted a bathtub shot. I wanted our friends and family to see the same luminous smiles and radiant blue eyes that I am privileged to gaze at every day. But someone was always too resistant, too tired, or too rambunctious.

One night we began finger painting a birthday card for my boys' Papa. Pretty soon shirts were off and paint was everywhere. Even the baby was getting slimed by his big brothers. I grabbed the camera. Bare-chested and paint-streaked boys weren't the image I had in mind, but the grins were big and the moment was quite reflective of where we were right then: joyful, creative, overwhelmed, and mom outnumbered by four men in the house. We had our card.

Days after the cards were in the mail, I was snapping a picture for something else, and in painless seconds had that "ideal" shot I'd originally been seeking for our Christmas cards. I wanted to jump inside the mailbox and start over. I could practically feel God grinning at a lesson learned, his Spirit reminding me that I can get wrongfully caught up in how the world sees my kids and my mothering. Easy to do, I suppose, with more media messages and how-to books and opportunities for our kids than ever before. We want to do this mom thing right. And it's hard to know what right is.

What really matters is who we are—in the luminous moments and the stinky ones. What matters is how we react to a struggle or a challenge and that we find other women we can share them with.

"You can't be true to who you are if you have to hide it to be in a relationship," my friend Noell said she's learned after ten years of mothering.

"Being authentic is something I've struggled with for many years," Toni said. "I thought if I didn't let people know the real me, it wouldn't hurt as bad when they moved on. But I got to a point in my life when I had lots of surface friendships but no really deep ones. To get to those deep, lifelong friendships meant I had to break down walls and share my true self. This is an area where I hope to teach my children well.

I want them to always be who they are, secure in themselves."

In the years to come you will have mommy moments that scar you and scare you, and hopefully you can eventually laugh at them. One day in church I laid my sleeping baby back in his car seat and chose not to interrupt his nap by buckling him in. I covered him with a blanket and carried him upstairs, then downstairs, and finally to the car. I stopped at a grocery store and was walking hurriedly through the parking lot when the seat got instantly lighter. I had unwittingly flopped my three-month-old onto concrete in full view of a bank of pay phones—each one occupied by a man. Mortified doesn't begin to cover how I felt. I didn't put my baby down for six hours.

I also had an elevator door close with my toddler alone inside. My husband let one of our sleeping babies roll off his lap in an airplane, as he too dozed off. Many friends have bumped over their children who have slipped out under the snack tray of their stroller. And I don't know a single mom who hasn't pushed her child's nap schedule to the point of a meltdown at least once.

We all make mistakes. The point is you must give yourself the grace you give your child. You are learning. Don't hide that beautiful process as you seek to form a new community of friends and as you seek to establish your parenting style. You don't know it all, and you never will. You will, though, grow to know your child.

"Seven years and three kids from starting this journey, I am still getting to know who these little people in my house are," Susan says. "I'm still learning to appreciate them."

The same could be said of getting to know yourself as a mom.

"Being 'real' for me is starting with myself," Julie says. "When I am honest with myself first, it is then easier to be honest and real with others. How much can I truly handle this week? What are the important activities for me to accomplish today? What are the end results I want for me, my marriage, and my children?"

It's through that kind of authenticity that we can raise kids to do their best, not pull their hair out at imperfection. It's by being real that we can make friends who enjoy surfing the waves of toddlerhood with us. It's by accepting ourselves and our shortcomings that we can cultivate family relationships that strengthen us, not make us feel small.

Build that village, strong and real. And in turn it will strengthen you.

Acknowledgments

From Susan

Thank you to the dozens of women who shared with me their ups and downs, moments of great triumph and great disgust, and the yearning and yelling in their hearts. You elevate the calling of motherhood by your intense love, dedication, and authenticity.

MOPS has enhanced mothering around the world and now across generations. I am confident, and deeply grateful, that its ripple effects will be felt throughout my family tree. Beth Lagerborg, thank you for asking me to dwell with you in God's perfect timing.

Thank you to Dr. Monica Reed for reviewing this project for medical relevance and accuracy and for her dedication to women's health.

This book was possible because of women I love and was written for women I don't know, including the ones who will one day love my boys. Zach, Luke, and A.J., you are life's most amazing gifts and most humbling projects. Todd, your love inspires me. Our journey with them and with God is transforming my heart. Thank you for never giving up on my becoming a mom.

From Monica

I would like to acknowledge the team at MOPS International—Mary Beth Lagerborg, Carla Foote, and Jean Blackmer—who extended the opportunity to me to be involved in this wonderful "labor" of love; Lee Hough with Alive Communications—who continues to be an ardent supporter; and last but not least my husband, my children, and my God—all of whom make my life a wonder-filled adventure.

MOPS

A Place to Belong

My son was six months old when I attended my first Mothers of Preschoolers meeting. I knew one person in a room of 130. I was clueless about mothering and about MOPS.

Six years later, I can hardly imagine one without the other. I'm a better mother, wife, friend, leader, and Christian for the words I've heard and the women I've met. Sitting with other mothers twice a month simply elevated the calling of motherhood for me. I laughed a lot, made many friends, and deepened my understanding of the privilege and promise it is to be a mom.

"It's very hard for me to allow someone else to peek behind my curtain. That said, MOPS has really opened my eyes to the fact that women can be real and share without losing face. I have become more compassionate toward others and less judgmental. It's true also for my role as a mother, being better able to extend an umbrella of grace over my children."

Susan

"I think the big
turning point in my life
was joining a moms group.
It saved me, being able to ask,
'Is your kid's poop green too?'"

Elizabeth

"After Macie's birth I hit a patch of depression. I had no family near and I knew no one since our move two weeks before her birth. It was all extremely overwhelming. My husband was busy with his new job and meeting new people, but I didn't have the energy or courage to venture out. But I signed up for MOPS, and it was my little light at the end of the tunnel. I met other moms with the same issues—kid struggles, marital strife just after having a baby, total exhaustion. It felt so good to have friends and feel like I belonged. I always felt good walking into MOPS meetings, even after a struggle taking the kids to child care. I finally felt like smiling again."

Stacie

MOPS began in 1973 with eight women coming together to talk, eat, share child care expenses, have a craft demonstration, and hear a short devotional. Three decades later this format lives on, with more than 100,000 women served in 4,000 groups—130 of them spread among more than 30 foreign countries. Some groups number just a handful of women; others break 100.

When it comes to creating a network of mom friends, MOPS is a no-brainer.

You might be thinking, *I'm not a joiner* or *I don't like big groups*. Here's the good news for you: MOPS breaks down big groups, and even small ones, into small tables of women who sit together for the year. They eat brunch together, discuss each speaker, plan girl's nights and park dates, celebrate life's highs, and empathize with each other's lows.

I am unabashed in my belief that MOPS changes the world by encouraging moms vocationally and

"Whether it's MOPS, or Mom to Mom, or another group, I need that validation and socialization, that sense of purpose. Hardly anyone admits how tough motherhood is. We all know it but we don't say it. It's good to have a place to be honest about it."

Angela

"Before I started MOPS, I had no idea how incredible motherhood and womanhood could be. I was just going through the motions. I thought more about the unnecessary details of mothering than about the really important aspects, like raising my boys to love the Lord and trusting God with their lives. Women can really be incredible to one another. At one time I thought that as a mother I could do nothing for anybody else but my children. When I came to MOPS, women with five children were making each other meals during hard times, watching each other's children, and taking the time to write incredible, uplifting notes to one another. I thought, WOW! I can be more than a mom! MOPS has changed the course of my life completely."

Tracy

spiritually as they influence the next generation. Here's my husband's opinion: "A hugely impactful thing," he says of MOPS. "I can always tell it's a MOPS Thursday because you've usually been inspired by what you've done, what you've heard, or who you've been with." (He's too private to tell you MOPS has benefited our marriage too, with all the candid speakers on relationships and intimacy.)

Stacia recognizes the same thing: "I joined for selfish reasons—time for me—and it ended up benefiting our whole family," she recalls.

Dana says MOPS impacts her every day. She has a will and her affairs in order thanks to one speaker. She is tremendously cautious about letting her son go to a public restroom alone, thanks to a safety speaker. Her children have chores, thanks to another presentation. And her filing system came as the result of hearing a speaker on organization.

"MOPS for me has been a little piece of heaven. Who knew I would find joy in sharing laundry stories and advice on what toilet brush works best? Who knew I would find myself sharing my world with no closed doors? By having an open heart and being authentic, women can really grow and learn from each other."

Hollie

Each of these women represents thousands just like you, who thrive in such an encouraging and empowering environment. For more information and to find a MOPS group close to you, check out the MOPS website at www.MOPS.org.

Susan Besze Wallace was a newspaper reporter for twelve years coast to coast, most recently with the *Denver Post*, before leaving to focus on the daily deadlines of sons Zach, Luke, and A.J. She led one of the largest MOPS (Mothers of Preschoolers) groups in the country and is a contributor to *MOMSense* magazine. Susan and husband Todd recently transplanted their busy brood to northern Virginia, where she continues writing freelance news stories and celebrating the roller coaster of motherhood in print.

Dr. Monica Reed is a physician, author, and speaker and has dedicated her life to promoting health, healing, and wellness. She currently serves as CEO of Florida Hospital Celebration Health. Dr. Reed is the author of *Creation Health Breakthrough: 8 Essentials to Revolutionize Your Health Physically, Mentally and Spiritually*. She and her husband Stanton Reed have two daughters: Melanie and Megan.

Better together...

MOPS is here to come alongside you
during this season of early mothering to
give you the support and resources you
need to be a great mom.

Get connected today!

Mothers of Preschoolers

2370 S. Trenton Way, Denver CO 80231
888.910.MOPS • **www.MOPS.org/bettermoms**

Perfect Gifts for a New Mom!

New moms run into a host of new challenges once baby arrives. *The New Mom's Guides* go straight to the heart of these matters, offering moms guidance and encouragement in this new season of life.